W9-BGJ-936

Just the Facts
Diabetes

Jenny Bryan

Heinemann Library
Chicago, Illinois

Customer Service 888-454-2279
Visit our website at www.heinemannlibrary.com

Produced by Monkey Puzzle Media
Designed by Jane Hawkins
Originated by Ambassador Litho Ltd.
Printed and bound in China by South China Printing Company

08 07 06 05 04
10 9 8 7 6 5 4 3 2 1

Library of Congress Cataloging-in-Publication Data
Bryan, Jenny.
  Diabetes / Jenny Bryan.
     p. cm. -- (Just the facts)
Summary: Discusses the two types of diabetes, causes of this disease,treatments available, and a variety of issues
surrounding this serious health concern.
Includes bibliographical references and index.
  ISBN 1-4034-4600-8 (Library Binding-hardcover)
  1. Diabetes--Juvenile literature. [1. Diabetes. 2. Diseases.] I.
Title. II. Series.
  RC660.5.B795 2003
  616.4'62--dc21
                          2003010910

Acknowledgments
The author and publisher are grateful to the following for permission to reproduce copyright material: front cover
(Amanda Knapp), pp. 17 (Richard Walker), 38, 43, 44 (Fotex Medien Agentur) Rex Features; pp. 1 (Russell D. Curtis), 4
(BSIP Estiot), 25 (John Bavosi), 27 (Russell D. Curtis), 32 (Western Opthalmic Hospital), 33 (BSIP Laurent), 36 (Cordelia
Molloy), 37 (Saturn Stills) Science Photo Library; pp. 5, 13, 18, 20, 21, 40 (Image Works) Topham Picturepoint; p. 6 AKG
London; pp. 7 (Bettmann), 23 (Arne Hodalic) Corbis; pp. 9, 10 Hulton Archive; p. 12 (Joff Lee) Anthony Blake Picture
Library; pp. 14–15 (Taxi) , 22 (Image Bank), 34 (Stone), 39 (Image Bank) Getty; p. 28 (Leo Mason) Action Plus; pp. 29, 49
Diabetes UK Picture Library; p. 30 Alamy; p. 47 Roslin Institute; p. 50 (Tony Adamson) Still Pictures.

Cover photograph: main: Corbis/LWA-JDC; second: Science Photo Library/Cordelia Molloy

The cover of this book shows a blood-glucose-level testing kit. For more information on why people with diabetes must
check their blood-glucose levels, turn to pages 36–37.

Special thanks to Pamela G. Richards, M.Ed., and Kate Campbell, diabetes nurse specialist manager,
for their help in the preparation of this book.

The case studies in this book are based on factual information. In some case studies and elsewhere in this book,
names or other personal information may have been changed or omitted in order to protect the privacy of the
individuals concerned.

Contents

The Diabetes Epidemic

Diabetes is much more common than it was twenty years ago. By 2010, it will affect about 220 million people around the world. Diabetes is the fifth leading cause of death in the United States.

People with diabetes have too much glucose in their bloodstream. Glucose is a type of sugar in food that everyone needs for energy. People with diabetes cannot convert it properly into energy because their bodies cannot make or cannot use a key substance, insulin.

Insulin is a hormone made in a gland called the pancreas, a banana-sized organ that lies across the back of the stomach. It helps glucose get into cells where it can be broken down for energy or stored.

Types of diabetes

There are two main types of diabetes: type 1 and type 2. Type 1 diabetes is most common in young people. At an early age, their pancreas stops making insulin.

You cannot feel your pancreas through your skin. Doctors use scanners to look at it.

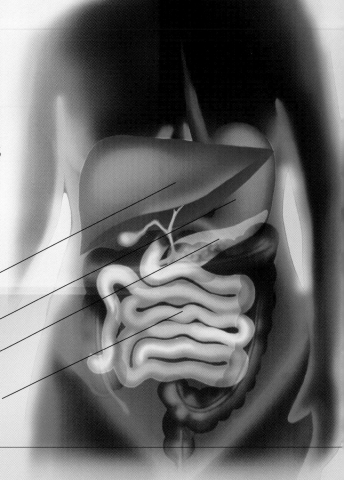

Liver

Stomach

Pancreas

Intestines

Type 2 diabetes used to occur only in middle-aged and elderly people. But it is now starting to affect people in their 20s and 30s, and even some teenagers. The pancreas still makes some insulin, but their body does not use it properly. Glucose levels build up in the blood instead of being broken down and turned into energy.

The main reason that type 2 diabetes is growing more common is that many people are becoming overweight. A big effort is needed to change the way people take care of themselves.

The cost of diabetes

Both type 1 and type 2 diabetes can be treated with diet and drugs. But having too much glucose in the blood for a long time gradually damages important parts of the body, including blood vessels and nerves.

Diabetes not only makes people ill, it costs countries a lot of money. Some people with diabetes need expensive treatment and have to stay in a hospital. This is why governments need to do something about the diabetes epidemic.

Healthy meals can taste good and help you avoid becoming overweight.

The History of Diabetes

Egyptian doctors described diabetes as early as 1500 B.C.E., according to an ancient piece of papyrus found in Luxor, Upper Egypt, in 1872. They also had a treatment for it that included beer swill, cucumber flower, and pond water.

But it was not until about 250 B.C.E. that Apollonius of Memphis, Egypt, is believed to have named the disease *diabetes.* Meaning "to go through," the name shows that physicians understood that people with the disease were getting rid of more fluid than they could drink. Great thirst and a need to urinate frequently are two of the common symptoms of diabetes.

In 500 C.E., two Indian doctors, Susruta and Charuka, discovered that urine produced by people with diabetes was sweet and sugary. It was sweet because of the glucose in it. But the disease did not get its full name— *diabetes mellitus*—until later, in Roman times. *Mellitus* is the Latin word for "honey," which is very sweet.

Early treatments

Over the next 900 years, physicians treated people with diabetes with some extraordinary treatments, including herbs and bleeding. To bleed a person, a doctor cut the patient or used leeches to draw out the blood.

At one point, Greek physicians prescribed exercise, preferably on horseback, to reduce patients' need to urinate. As late as the 17th century, a leading medical text suggested eating powdered mouse (with fleas) for treating diabetes!

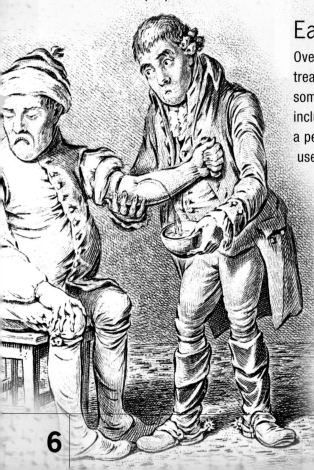

Removing blood from a vein used to be a common treatment.

Famous people who have or had diabetes

- Novelist H. G. Wells, author of *The Time Machine, The Invisible Man,* and other books
- Menachem Begin, prime minister of Israel
- American country musician Johnny Cash
- American jazz singer Ella Fitzgerald
- French impressionist painter Paul Cézanne
- American businessperson Howard Hughes
- American tennis player Arthur Ashe
- American boxer Sugar Ray Robinson
- British Olympic rower Sir Steve Redgrave
- American actress Halle Berry

Sugar Ray Robinson, an American professional boxer who was a world champion six times, suffered from diabetes.

The pancreas

With so much emphasis on the sugary urine of people with diabetes, doctors assumed it was a disease of the kidneys—the organs in the body that clean the blood and produce urine. It was not until late in the 18th century that researchers discovered that the blood of people with diabetes was also sugary. They rightly concluded that diabetes was a disease that affected the whole body.

In 1869 anatomist Paul Langerhans identified the key cells in the pancreas, now called the islets of Langerhans, that are known to produce the main substance that controls glucose levels in the body. Twenty years later, two German researchers made the connection between the pancreas and diabetes. When they removed the pancreas of some dogs, the animals developed diabetes.

The discovery of insulin

Once they realized that the islets of Langerhans were the key to diabetes, early 20th-century researchers worked to extract the key ingredient, insulin, that controls glucose levels in the body. However, they soon found that this was much more difficult than they had expected.

The pancreas does not just make insulin, it also makes enzymes to digest food in the intestines. At first, scientists could not extract insulin without these enzymes. As soon as the mixture was in a test tube, the enzymes digested the insulin.

Banting and Best

In 1920 Canadian doctor Frederick Banting came up with the idea of tying off parts of the pancreas in order to kill the cells that produced digestive enzymes, without damaging the islets of Langerhans.

Working with a colleague, Charles Best, Banting gradually improved his technique for extracting insulin from the pancreas. The pair tested their insulin on dogs with diabetes and found they were able to control the animals' glucose levels. Realizing the importance of the research, other scientists at the University of Toronto joined Banting and Best in extracting and purifying the insulin.

Dramatic results

In early 1922, the first patient with diabetes was injected with a small amount of insulin. Leonard Thompson was fourteen years old. Until then, he had been kept alive by the "starvation diet" that was sometimes used to treat people with diabetes at that time. As a result of the diet, he weighed only 66 pounds (30 kilograms) when he was treated with Banting and Best's new pancreatic extract.

The first injection had only a small effect. But when Leonard was injected with a purer extract of insulin some weeks later, the results were dramatic. The amount of glucose in his blood fell and he soon started to gain weight and strength. Other patients were treated with increasingly refined samples of insulin with similar positive results.

Banting and Best pioneered insulin therapy for treatment of diabetes.

A prize-winning achievement

Within a few years, insulin became widely available. In 1923 Banting was awarded the Nobel Prize for Medicine, an important international award, because his research was considered so important. In 1934 he was given the title "Sir." Seven years later, however, he was killed in an airplane crash in Newfoundland.

After insulin

Before the discovery of insulin, a child with type 1 diabetes would live only a few weeks. A middle-aged adult diagnosed with type 2 diabetes would die within ten years. By 1945, when insulin was widely available, there had been a big improvement. A newly diagnosed 10-year-old could expect to live until about 45 or 50, and a 50-year-old until he or she was about 65. Today, people with diabetes still live five to ten fewer years than people who do not have the condition. But they lead much healthier and more normal lives than those who had diabetes 100 or even 50 years ago.

After the initial successes with insulin, researchers found ways to make a dose of treatment work longer in the body, so that people with diabetes did not need to inject themselves so often.

Making insulin in a factory in 1946. The purified insulin flows out at the bottom into the bucket.

Genetic engineering

Until the 1970s, people injected themselves with insulin taken from the pancreas of cattle or pigs. Then came a big breakthrough for many modern insulin users, when scientists found a way to produce human insulin by genetic engineering. This involves putting the gene that controls normal insulin production in the human pancreas into bacterial cells. The gene is activated so that the bacteria make insulin. Some people still find that they respond better to animal insulin. But the genetically engineered human insulin is better for many.

New treatments

There were also new treatments for people with type 2 diabetes, starting with drugs called sulfonylureas in the 1950s. In the second half of the 20th century, the differences between type 1 and type 2 diabetes became clearer.

For example, researchers called type 1 diabetes an autoimmune disease. This is a disease in which the cells that normally defend the body from infection start to attack other cells in the body. In type 1 diabetes, these cells attack the islets of Langerhans.

By finding out more about the causes of type 1 and type 2 diabetes, scientists were able to tailor treatment more accurately to the different types of diabetes.

Good glucose control

In 1993 doctors discovered that people with type 1 diabetes who kept the amount of glucose in their blood under control had the fewest health problems. By testing their blood regularly and using medication to keep their glucose at near-normal levels, they had fewer complications than people who were less careful. Their heart and other organs, blood vessels, and nerves were in better shape. A further study, published in 1998, confirmed that the same was true for people with type 2 diabetes.

As a result of this research, people with diabetes are encouraged to check their blood-glucose levels regularly and adapt their treatment according to the results.

Type 1 Diabetes

Type 1 diabetes is sometimes called insulin-dependent diabetes or juvenile-onset diabetes. It occurs when a person's body cannot make the hormone insulin.

Insulin helps to convert glucose into energy in cells all over the body. The body gets its glucose by digesting starchy, carbohydrate foods in the diet, such as bread, potatoes, pasta, and rice. The glucose in these foods is absorbed from the intestine into the bloodstream.

During a meal, the pancreas makes insulin. Insulin is then released into the bloodstream where it helps glucose get out of the blood and into cells. Once the glucose is inside the cells, it acts as fuel to provide the body with energy or it is sent for storage in muscle and liver cells.

Symptoms of diabetes

Without insulin, people with type 1 diabetes are unable to use the carbohydrates and sugar in their food properly. This makes them begin to feel sick. Some of the symptoms they get occur with other illnesses, too. When several of these symptoms are present at once, it is a sign that it could be diabetes.

A very common symptom of diabetes is feeling thirsty, not just after playing sports or when it is hot, but all the time. People need to drink a lot, and then they need to urinate frequently, too.

Another symptom is feeling very tired. This is because people with diabetes cannot get enough energy from the glucose in their food. It is not just the fatigue people feel after a busy day. They feel tired nearly all the time, even after a good night's sleep or without doing anything very active.

Starchy foods like bread and potatoes are good sources of energy.

Diabetes also makes people lose weight, since they do not get enough nourishment from their food. It is not like the effects of dieting. They seem to be eating enough but they just get thinner.

Infections

Too much glucose in the bloodstream can lead to fungal infection. There are many different types of fungi, not just mushrooms and toadstools. One type of fungal infection, called thrush, looks a bit like cottage cheese. In people who are ill, including those with diabetes, thrush can grow in many different parts of the body.

"I'd had the typical diabetes symptoms—hunger, thirst, weight loss, fatigue, and going to the bathroom as though it was my new best friend. I remember my mom taking me to the doctor and having a urine and blood test done. I really had no idea what was going on. When the doctor told me I had diabetes I didn't really think it was such a big deal because I'd never even heard of it until that day!"

(Dani, fourteen-year-old who has diabetes, www.childrenwithdiabetes.com)

Type 2 Diabetes

Type 2 diabetes tends to develop more slowly than type 1 diabetes. The cells in the islets of Langerhans that make insulin do not suddenly fail. Instead, they gradually deteriorate, and the body does not respond properly to the insulin that the islet cells make.

Insulin resistance

Cells, particularly in the muscles, liver, and fat, develop insulin resistance. They can no longer use insulin to get glucose into their cells, so glucose levels rise in the bloodstream. The islets of Langerhans try to make up for this by producing more insulin. For a while, there are higher than average levels of the hormone in the blood. But eventually, the islet cells get worn out and produce less and less insulin.

Rise in type 2 diabetes

At one time, type 2 diabetes was called maturity-onset diabetes since it only started (the onset) in middle-aged and elderly (mature) people.

❝Television viewing is thought to promote weight gain not only by displacing physical activity, but also by increasing energy intake . . . U.S. and British children are exposed to about ten food commercials per hour of television time . . . most for fast food, soft drinks, sweets, and sugar-sweetened breakfast cereal.❞

(Cara B. Ebbeling, Dorota B. Pawlak, David S. Ludwig, *The Lancet* medical journal, 2002)

But it is now affecting much younger people, including teenagers and young adults.

Type 2 diabetes is sometimes called mild diabetes. But it is just as serious as type 1 diabetes. The symptoms are similar to those of type 1 diabetes, but they may build up more slowly. The long-term damage to blood vessels, nerves, eyes, and major organs can be just as serious as with type 1 diabetes.

Diabetes specialists are very concerned about the rise in type 2 diabetes in younger people. They are linking it to the big increase in the number of teenagers and young adults who are overweight or obese.

Diet and exercise

Young people eat more sweet and fatty foods than their parents and grandparents did at their age. There are many more of these foods to choose from, especially snack foods like burgers, fries, cookies, and sweets, and there are more places to buy them.

Children and teenagers also get less exercise than previous generations. Far fewer walk to school and they play fewer sports. Instead, they tend to relax by hanging out with their friends, watching TV, or playing computer games. All this means that they use up less energy, and more of the food they eat is converted into fat.

It's fine for these young people to relax, as long as they exercise and eat sensibly, too.

IGT

Before people develop type 2 diabetes, they usually go through a phase in which their body does not handle glucose as efficiently as it should. They do not have diabetes yet, but they are starting to show signs of insulin resistance. This phase is called impaired glucose tolerance (IGT), or pre-diabetes.

People with IGT do not need the same treatment as those with diabetes. But they can take steps to reduce their risk of developing the disease. Many are overweight and eat too many sweet and fatty foods. They might not get enough exercise.

No symptoms

People with impaired glucose tolerance do not usually have any symptoms, so they are unlikely to go to their doctor for help. But a growing number of diabetes specialists support the idea of national screening programs to test the blood-glucose levels of people who are at high risk of IGT.

People with close relatives with diabetes are more likely to have IGT than those who do not have a family history. People who are overweight or have high blood pressure or other signs of heart disease are also more likely to have IGT.

"We are now in the process of changing the public health message to say to doctors they not only need to do a better job caring for diabetes, but they have to find people at high risk and they need to do something about the onset of diabetes. That is a . . . lot to ask a doctor or a nurse to do."

(Frank Vinicor, diabetes program director for the U.S. Centers for Disease Control and Prevention, *Philadelphia Inquirer*, August 12, 2002)

If the people at risk of IGT were given blood tests, doctors could find out if they were in this pre-diabetes stage. Blood-glucose levels in people with IGT are not as high as in those with diabetes, but they are higher than normal. Finding out they had IGT would give people time to change their diet, lose weight, exercise more, and reduce their risk before they developed diabetes.

Setting up these types of tests costs a lot of money, so there are not many of these screening programs. Most people do not realize they have a problem until they are diagnosed with diabetes.

Playing sports can help control your weight and help you avoid IGT and diabetes.

The Rise of Diabetes

The continuing rise of diabetes in both developed and developing countries appears unstoppable. In 1985 it was estimated that about 30 million people around the world had diabetes. By 2000, only 15 years later, the figure had risen to over 150 million. The World Health Organization predicts that by 2025, the number of people with diabetes will have almost doubled, to about 300 million.

The largest increase is likely to be in developing countries in Africa and Southeast Asia rather than in developed regions, such as the United States and Europe. The big rise in diabetes has been in type 2, not type 1 diabetes, and nine out of ten cases of diabetes are now type 2.

Spending the day at a desk does not use much energy. Lack of exercise can lead to a weight problem and diabetes.

There are two main reasons for the alarming increase in diabetes:

- More people are living longer and reaching an age at which the risk of type 2 diabetes increases.
- Many people eat too much, especially sweet and fatty fast foods or junk foods. They are also less active. This means that more people are becoming overweight and obese and are increasing their risk of developing type 2 diabetes.

Urbanization

All over the world, lifestyles are changing and many people have diets different than their parents and grandparents. Many are moving to cities in search of work. They may spend all day sitting in offices instead of doing physical labor like farming. Some people snack throughout the day —at their desk, in the shopping mall, or in the car—instead of sitting down to regular meals at home. Diabetes tends to be an urban disease, and as urbanization spreads across the globe, diabetes is growing with it.

Worldwide diabetes statistics

In 2000, the five countries with the largest numbers of people with diabetes were:

- India 32.7 million (population 1 billion)
- China 22.6 million (population 1.275 billion)
- United States 15.3 million (population 283 million)
- Pakistan 8.8 million (population 141 million)
- Japan 7.1 million (population 127 million).

Europe has 26.5 million people with diabetes.

The five countries with the highest rates of the disease were: Papua New Guinea (15.5%), Mauritius (15.0%), Bahrain (14.8%), Mexico (14.2%), and Trinidad & Tobago (14.1%).

(International Diabetes Federation; population figures from United Nations Population Division)

Cultural Factors

Some ethnic groups are more likely to develop diabetes, especially type 2 diabetes, than others. Among them are African Americans, Native Americans, and South Asian people. In the United States, for example, African Americans are twice as likely to have diabetes as non-Hispanic whites. A quarter of African Americans between the ages of 65 and 74 have diabetes.

The ethnic groups that are most likely to have diabetes may have genes that increase their risk, but no one is sure what the genes are. Economic factors could be important, too. Groups with relatively high levels of poverty, such as African Americans in the United States, tend to eat a poor diet and have more health problems than wealthier groups.

Informing people

Changing their diet to reduce the amount of sweet and fatty foods that they eat, getting more exercise, and taking better care of their health can all help reduce people's risk of developing diabetes, whatever their cultural origins.

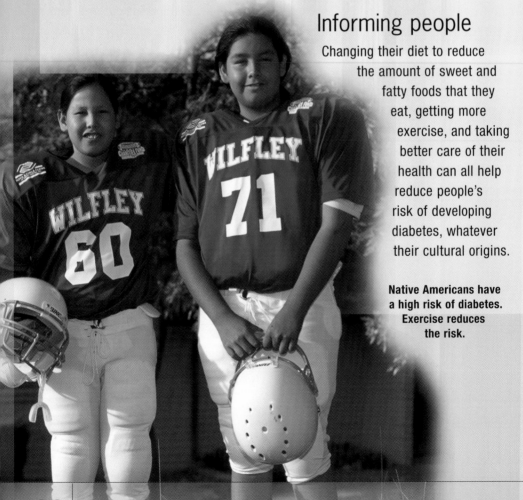

Native Americans have a high risk of diabetes. Exercise reduces the risk.

But some people may not realize how important these things are, especially if they do not speak or cannot read the language of the country in which they are living. They may not be able to afford to see health-care workers who can test them for diabetes and explain how to treat the condition. They may miss out on regular checkups for complications.

Simply translating information sheets into languages that people can understand is not enough. Getting the message across about the importance of a healthy lifestyle and effective diabetes treatment involves more than that. People need to trust the doctor or nurse who is trying to help them before they will accept their advice. This takes time and commitment from everyone—patients, their families, and health-care workers.

Fasting

Doctors advise people with diabetes who want to observe religious festivals involving fasting, such as Ramadan, to seek medical advice before they start. During Ramadan, Muslims do not eat anything from sunrise to sunset. But this can be difficult for people with diabetes.

They will need to change the dose of their medication and, if they have problems with their blood-glucose levels, they may need to stop fasting. Religious leaders are very understanding of the health needs of people with certain conditions, such as diabetes, for whom fasting may be dangerous. They can advise people how to avoid damaging their health.

Muslims with diabetes can get medical advice about fasting safely during Ramadan.

Diabetes in Pregnancy

Some women are diagnosed with diabetes when they are pregnant. This is called gestational diabetes. If it happens during the first twelve weeks of the pregnancy, it probably means that a woman had diabetes before she became pregnant. If it starts at a later stage of the pregnancy, it is more likely due to the fact that she cannot make enough insulin to meet her own needs and that of her baby.

Some women are more likely to develop diabetes during pregnancy than others, such as:

- overweight women
- those with a family history of type 2 diabetes
- women who had a very large baby in a previous pregnancy
- women whose baby died without any clear reason in a previous pregnancy.

Women with gestational diabetes may be able to bring down their blood-glucose levels by eating regularly and sticking to low-sugar, low-fat, healthy foods. But others need insulin to control their blood sugar while they are pregnant.

Eating healthy is especially important during pregnancy. Women with gestational diabetes should take extra care.

Future health problems

Gestational diabetes usually goes away after the baby is born. But women who have had gestational diabetes are three times more likely to develop type 2 diabetes at some time in their life than those who have not had diabetes during pregnancy.

Pregnancy and diabetes among the Pima

The highest levels of diabetes in the world are found in the Pima, a Native American people of Arizona. Over half of the Pima who live on U.S. reservations develop type 2 diabetes. They may have genes that put them at risk. Also, the Pima tend to eat an unhealthy diet and not exercise regularly. This makes things worse.

Recent research has suggested that exposure to high glucose levels in the womb also plays a role. Seven out of ten Pima children whose mothers had diabetes when they were pregnant go on to develop diabetes as young adults.

This could be significant for all women with diabetes. Type 2 diabetes used to affect older women who already had children. But, as more women get type 2 diabetes when they are young and able to become pregnant, more babies will be exposed to high glucose levels in the womb. This increases their risk of getting diabetes in later life.

This Pima man lives on a reservation in the United States.

Genetic Links

Both type 1 and type 2 diabetes run in families. Often, several people in a family have the condition. Research suggests that they have inherited genes from their parents that have made them more likely to get diabetes than other people.

Several genes seem to be involved in diabetes, and this makes it difficult to determine the real cause of the problem. Scientists think that faulty genes alone are not enough to give people diabetes. Environmental factors are probably at work, too. People may inherit genes that increase their risk of getting diabetes. But they may then be exposed to something that changes the way these genes work before they actually develop diabetes.

Diabetes genes

In type 2 diabetes, eating too many sugary and fatty foods and becoming overweight may somehow activate diabetes genes and cause people to develop the condition.

Type 1 diabetes starts much earlier than type 2 diabetes. The genes may be affected by something that a child is exposed to in the first few years of life or even earlier in the womb, before he or she is born. This could be high blood-glucose levels in the mother's bloodstream during pregnancy or it could be exposure to infection at a young age.

Infections

Young children get many minor infections, with no lasting effects. But children with genes for diabetes may respond differently to infection. Their immune systems could somehow start to attack the islets of Langerhans in the pancreas, instead of just protecting them from harmful microbes.

Studying twins

Many studies have been done to try to identify the diabetes genes and other possible causes of the condition. Researchers often study identical twins with diabetes in the family because they have exactly the same genes. If it were genes alone that caused diabetes, then either both twins would inherit the genes and develop the condition or neither twin would inherit the genes and get diabetes. But that does not happen. Often, one twin gets diabetes and the other does not.

So researchers look for differences in the way the children have grown up. They look at different infections they have had and any differences in diet and lifestyle. They look for anything that may have somehow activated the diabetes genes of one twin but not the other and that could be a clue to what triggers diabetes in other people, too.

An islet of Langerhans is pictured below. In a healthy pancreas, cells in the islets produce insulin.

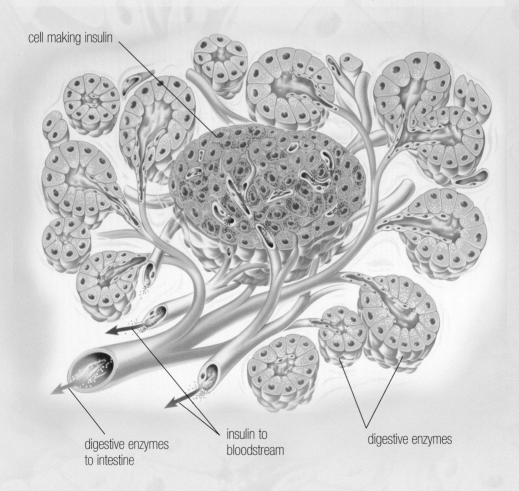

cell making insulin

digestive enzymes to intestine

insulin to bloodstream

digestive enzymes

Treating Diabetes

Type 1 diabetes

Anyone with type 1 diabetes needs insulin injections to replace the hormones not produced in the pancreas. The treatment is designed to keep blood-glucose levels controlled, as if the insulin was being produced naturally. This means increasing the amount of insulin in the blood at mealtimes and reducing the amount between meals.

There are many different brands of insulin, and at present, they all have to be injected. Because insulin is a protein, scientists have never been able to make it into a tablet form.

The digestive juices in the stomach would break the protein down before it had a chance to do its job. But scientists are working on alternative methods of delivery, such as aerosols that allow the insulin to be inhaled.

Genetic engineering

Some people use insulins that are extracted from the pancreases of pigs and cattle, while others use human insulin that is made by genetic engineering. In this process, the gene which controls normal insulin production in the human pancreas is put into bacterial cells. There, it is activated so that the bacteria make

"The pump is not a cure (which is what I would really like), but it has made a lot of things so much easier. I can sleep in on the weekends and I can stay up late with my friends and have late-night snacks! There are even times when I am playing with my friends that I just skip a meal—especially lunch on the weekends, and that's OK, too. I don't have to stop what I am doing to have a snack or a meal. I eat what I want when I want."

(Brian, twelve-year-old who has diabetes, www.childrenwithdiabetes.com)

human insulin, something that they would not normally do. The insulin is then collected and purified.

Some brands of insulin work fast, while others take longer to kick in. There are types that work only for a few hours, others for much longer. Some people use one type of insulin to control their glucose levels between meals and also take a short-acting insulin at mealtimes. Alternatively, they can use a ready-made insulin mixture that contains some shorter-acting and some longer-acting insulin. A once-daily, long-acting brand of insulin that aims to provide steady glucose control throughout the day is also available.

People use insulin pumps to achieve good glucose control without regular injections.

Insulin pumps

Insulin pumps are the high-tech route to better glucose control for many people with type 1 diabetes. Worn on the outside of the body on a belt or in a pocket, the most sophisticated insulin pumps are about the size of a pager. They can be programmed to deliver insulin through a needle inserted under the skin, usually on the abdomen.

Between meals the device provides a low level of insulin around the clock. It also allows users to deliver a larger dose before meals, matched to the amount of food they will eat. They can also reduce the amount of insulin they are getting when they exercise, so their blood-glucose levels do not drop too low.

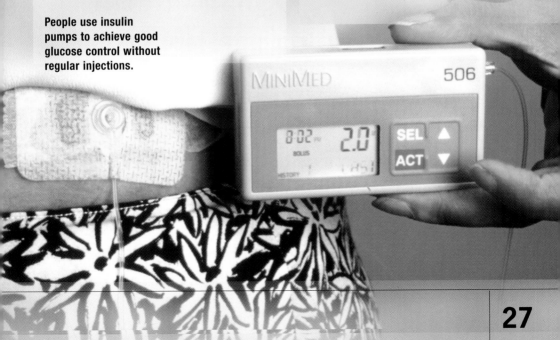

Type 2 diabetes

Since people with type 2 diabetes do make some insulin, they do not usually need insulin injections until they have had the illness for some time. Instead, the treatment in the early stages of the condition is aimed at improving the way their body responds to insulin.

Some people at this stage can control their blood-glucose levels by changing their diet and getting more exercise, especially if they are very overweight. People with type 2 diabetes are advised to exercise and to eat a healthy diet to keep their weight under control, even if they need drugs to treat their diabetes.

Drug treatments

There are several types of drugs for type 2 diabetes and, unlike insulin, they can all be taken as pills.

Sulfonylureas are the most widely prescribed drugs for type 2 diabetes. They cause islet cells in the pancreas to produce more insulin. However, they tend to make people gain weight, which can be a problem for people with type 2 diabetes who are already struggling to keep their weight down.

Metformin is the first choice of treatment for people who are overweight, since it does not make them gain weight. Some doctors prefer it for type 2 diabetes because medical research has shown that it can reduce the risk of complications from diabetes. It lowers blood-glucose levels by reducing the amount of glucose released from the liver and by improving

Many people with type 2 diabetes must remember to take several pills every day.

the way muscle and fat cells respond to insulin. The downside is that some people get an upset stomach when they take it.

Other drugs for type 2 diabetes are usually taken as an additional therapy when people with type 2 diabetes cannot control their glucose levels with a sulfonylurea or metformin on its own. Some can be taken just at mealtimes to boost insulin release with food.

Many drugs used to treat type 2 diabetes become less effective when people take them for long periods, because glucose levels rise over time. Some people develop unwanted side effects from using them, such as an upset stomach. Most people with type 2 diabetes will probably eventually need to use insulin along with other drugs.

Emergency!

The most common reason for a diabetic emergency is too little rather than too much sugar in the bloodstream. This is called hypoglycemia, or a hypo.

Hypoglycemia

Hypoglycemia usually occurs when people with diabetes have more insulin in their bloodstream than they need, so their blood-glucose levels drop too low.

This can happen if they have not eaten as much as they expected or if they have used up more energy than they planned.

The normal pancreas adapts to changes in routine. If lunch is late, it waits until there is food in the body before it releases insulin. But people who rely on insulin injections to control their glucose levels cannot be so flexible.

"I play sports like softball and some soccer and when I'm on the field I say 'TIME OUT, I'm low!' Then I drink a juice and eat some crackers and I'm pumped up as ever."

(Mallory, young person who has diabetes, www.childrenwithdiabetes.com)

It is important to know how to help a friend with diabetes if she or he has a hypo.

If they take their insulin or other diabetes medicine because they are about to eat, and then get called away and miss the meal, they can have problems. Once the medicine is in their bloodstream, they cannot get it out. Their glucose levels may fall too low.

Another common trigger for a hypo is when someone uses up more of the glucose in their bloodstream than they had planned by playing sports or going for a long walk.

Having a hypo

When people are having a hypo they can become confused and disoriented. They may slur their speech or become angry and behave strangely. If something is not done to help them, they may fall over and become unconscious. Doctors advise people who experience the first sign of a hypo to drink something sweet and then have a cookie or snack.

Some people with diabetes buy glucose gels and keep them with them at all times. If they have a hypo and are not able to swallow, someone can smear the gel on the inside of their mouth. This is a quick way to get glucose into their bloodstream.

Hypos do not have any lasting effects. After eating or drinking something sweet or using a glucose gel, a person usually feels better within ten to fifteen minutes and can continue as normal.

Taking special care

Having a hypo while driving or handling heavy machinery is dangerous, so people with diabetes need to take special care to check their blood-glucose levels regularly. They should not miss meals when they are on the road or working with machines.

Although hypos sound very scary, most people get used to recognizing the early warning symptoms and taking action.

Warning! Hypo!

Typical hypo warning signs are
- feeling panicky, hungry, wobbly, or confused
- tingling in the mouth and lips
- blurred eyesight
- sweating
- rapid heartbeat.

Complications

Thanks to modern treatments, few people in the developed world die as a direct result of high blood-glucose levels. But they do get complications that affect many parts of their body. Complications of diabetes result from the long-term effects of high blood-glucose levels on the blood vessels.

Diabetic retinopathy

Damage to the small blood vessels in the eye, called diabetic retinopathy, is the most frequent single complication of diabetes. It tends to affect people who have had diabetes for many years, especially if they have not controlled their glucose levels very successfully. The condition can lead to blindness.

Blocks, leaks, and swelling of the tiny blood vessels at the back of the eye can cause permanent damage to the retina. (This is the part of the eye where images are focused before they are sent to the brain.) Diabetes is the leading cause of blindness and poor vision in adults living in developed countries.

Leaky blood vessels in the eye caused by diabetes can damage the retina and lead to blindness. The large red area in the center of this picture is blood that has leaked inside the eye.

Kidneys and nerves

Similar damage to the small blood vessels in the kidneys can lead to kidney failure. The kidneys are vital organs that clean the blood, so people with kidney failure need their blood cleaned regularly by dialysis machines or require a kidney transplant.

Nerves also need a good blood supply to keep them healthy. If the blood vessels supplying them are affected by diabetes, extensive nerve damage can occur.

People with diabetes often face serious problems with their feet because of nerve damage. In extreme cases their feet or legs become so damaged that they have to be amputated. Diabetes is the most common cause of amputation that is not the result of an accident. People with diabetes are 15 to 40 times more likely to require a leg amputation compared to the population in general, although it is still uncommon.

Other complications

When high blood-glucose levels damage large blood vessels, this can lead to heart attacks or strokes, which may be fatal. Fifty percent of people with diabetes die as a result of heart disease, compared with about twenty percent of the general population.

In people with type 2 diabetes, complications start surprisingly early, often years before they even know they have the disease. This is why it is so important to diagnose and treat type 2 diabetes as early as possible.

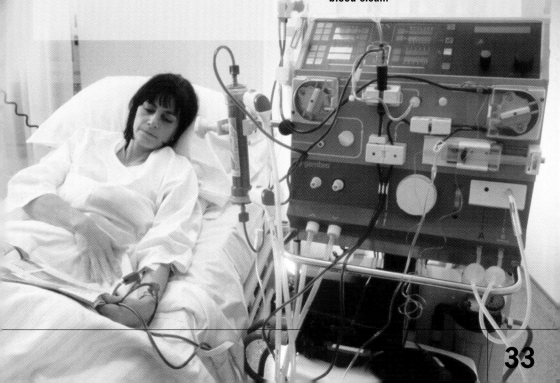

People with kidney failure need a dialysis machine to keep their blood clean.

33

Preventing Type 2 Diabetes

Diet and exercise

Diet and exercise have been shown to delay and possibly prevent people at high risk of getting type 2 diabetes from developing the condition. In 2001 results from a large U.S. study confirmed what diabetes specialists have thought for some time. Even if a person is overweight and blood-glucose levels are starting to go up, it may not be too late to avoid diabetes.

The Diabetes Prevention Program

More than 3,000 people took part in the Diabetes Prevention Program, sponsored by the National Institute of Diabetes and Digestive and Kidney Diseases, in the United States. They were as young as 25 and as old as 85. They were African Americans, white, Asian Americans, and Hispanic Americans. Some had a family history of diabetes, and some of the women had diabetes when they were pregnant. What they all had in common was that they were overweight and they had impaired glucose tolerance.

The cost of diabetes

The complications of diabetes, such as blindness, kidney failure, and heart disease, cost healthcare services a huge amount of money. Diabetes costs an estimated five to ten percent of a nation's health budget.

A third of the group went on the lifestyle program, a third took metformin to reduce their glucose levels, and a third did nothing (though they were given information about diet and exercise, as were those who took metformin). Those who took part in the lifestyle program were given special training about healthy eating and encouraged to exercise for 30 minutes each day. Most chose walking.

Results of the program

After three years, those who went on the lifestyle program had reduced their risk of getting type 2 diabetes by 58 percent and lost 5 to 7 percent of their body weight. Only 14 percent had developed diabetes during the study compared to 29 percent of those who did not take part in the lifestyle program. Of those who took metformin, 22 percent developed diabetes. The program suggests that a successful diet and exercise program is more effective at preventing diabetes than medication.

Exercise combined with good diet improves general health and can prevent diabetes.

"Every year a person can live free of diabetes means an added year of life free of pain, disability, and medical costs incurred by this disease."

(Dr. Allen Spiegel, director of the National Institute of Diabetes and Digestive and Kidney Diseases in the United States)

Regular Testing

An essential part of treatment for people with diabetes is testing the amount of glucose they have in their body. This lets them know if their blood-glucose levels are going too high or too low.

Urine tests

Tests can be done on both urine and blood. Urine tests are simple to do. A specially prepared stick or strip is dipped in a sample of urine and changes color according to the amount of glucose in the urine. However, in some people, glucose only starts to appear in their urine when the level in their blood is very high. So they may think their blood-glucose levels are fine and be unaware that they need to adapt their treatment. The other drawback of urine tests (which are not generally used by people with type 1 diabetes) is that they do not show when glucose levels are too low.

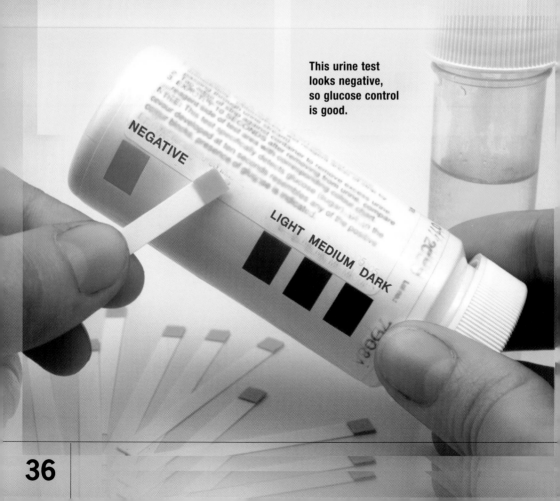

This urine test looks negative, so glucose control is good.

NEGATIVE

LIGHT MEDIUM DARK

This man is holding a glucose test strip against a scale to check his blood-glucose level.

Blood tests

Blood tests give a more accurate reading, and they show when glucose levels are too high or too low. The test can be done by pricking a finger to get a tiny sample of blood. The sample is put onto a strip and is read by a small monitor. This gives a precise measurement of the amount of glucose in the sample.

If the reading is low, the person will need to take some glucose, or have a sweet drink or something to eat, such as a sandwich or cookie. A single high reading on its own may not be a problem, especially if a person is not feeling ill. But if the level does not return to normal within a few hours, the dose of insulin may need to be changed.

Regular testing

Some people test their glucose level once or twice a day, while others test more often. They need to vary the time of day that they do the test to get a complete picture of how well their glucose levels are being controlled throughout the day. Regular testing also shows how much effect food and exercise are having on a particular individual's glucose and energy levels. It is important to record the results so that the person with diabetes, or the doctor, can check trends over a period of time.

Adapting Treatment to Lifestyle

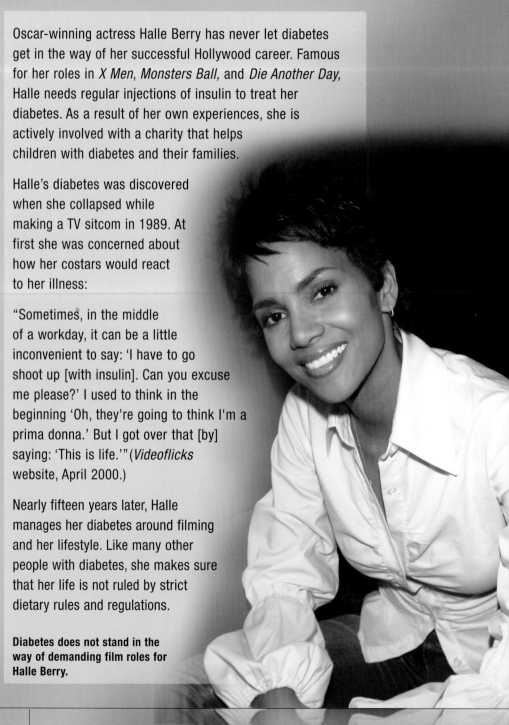

Oscar-winning actress Halle Berry has never let diabetes get in the way of her successful Hollywood career. Famous for her roles in *X Men*, *Monsters Ball,* and *Die Another Day*, Halle needs regular injections of insulin to treat her diabetes. As a result of her own experiences, she is actively involved with a charity that helps children with diabetes and their families.

Halle's diabetes was discovered when she collapsed while making a TV sitcom in 1989. At first she was concerned about how her costars would react to her illness:

"Sometimes, in the middle of a workday, it can be a little inconvenient to say: 'I have to go shoot up [with insulin]. Can you excuse me please?' I used to think in the beginning 'Oh, they're going to think I'm a prima donna.' But I got over that [by] saying: 'This is life.'" (*Videoflicks* website, April 2000.)

Nearly fifteen years later, Halle manages her diabetes around filming and her lifestyle. Like many other people with diabetes, she makes sure that her life is not ruled by strict dietary rules and regulations.

Diabetes does not stand in the way of demanding film roles for Halle Berry.

Blood-glucose control

By understanding the effects that typical daily activities have on their diabetes, a growing number of people with the condition are achieving good blood-glucose control without too many restrictions on what they do. Maintaining good blood-glucose control is about balancing energy intake with output, with a little help from antidiabetic medication.

People with diabetes are encouraged to eat regular, balanced meals and get plenty of exercise. If they need to miss a meal or they know they are going to eat later than usual, they may need to reduce or delay their dose of medication. In the same way, if they know they are going to work out in the gym or get some other strenuous exercise, they will need extra energy and need to adapt their treatment.

The aim is for people to change their treatment to suit their lifestyle. They need to be sure that they are keeping good control of their blood-glucose levels without risking a hypo. But they do not need to go without all the treats that other people enjoy.

Diet Myths

You may have heard that people with diabetes should not eat candy, cookies, cake, or other such foods that many of us enjoy. That is not true. People with diabetes can eat some sugary, high-calorie foods. But, like any other people who are trying to eat a balanced diet and control their weight, people with diabetes should not eat too many sweet and fatty foods.

Healthy eating

Healthy eating means eating regular meals, based on starchy foods such as bread, pasta, potatoes, and unsweetened breakfast cereals. Healthy eating also means eating at least five portions of fruit and vegetables each day. These not only contain vitamins. They are also high in fiber, which helps digestion and glucose absorption.

Healthy eating means cutting back on fatty foods and those that are cooked in oil, such as burgers and fries. Vegetable fats, when used for cooking, are better than animal fats. Baking or grilling food cuts down on the amount of oil in a typical meal. Eating chicken and fish rather than fatty red meat also reduces fat intake.

Making sensible choices

People with diabetes are advised to choose low-calorie drinks and foods with no added sugar, though they do not need to cut out sugar completely. Many products, such as fruit juice, use low amounts of sugar or alternative sweeteners. It should not be difficult to find brands that are healthful and taste good.

Some stores sell so-called diabetic brands that are specially designed for people with diabetes. Such foods became popular in the 1960s, when people with diabetes were advised to eat a sugar-free, low-carbohydrate diet. Diabetic foods usually contain sweeteners such as sorbitol or fructose. These sweeteners are not classed as sugars but, in fact, they act in the same way as sugars once they are in the body.

Experts now advise people with diabetes to choose low-fat, low-sugar brands of regular foods rather than pay higher prices for diabetic foods.

"Labeling candy and cookies as 'suitable for diabetics' undermines advice to people with diabetes to eat a healthy diet, high in carbohydrates like cereals, pasta, rice, and bread, including fruit and vegetables, but low in fat."

(Sir John Krebs, Chairman of the United Kingdom Food Standards Agency)

Living with Diabetes

Steve Redgrave's story

When top Olympic champion rower Steve Redgrave was diagnosed with type 2 diabetes, he thought his international career was over. His rowing depended on a very high level of fitness and good health. But his diabetes specialists and trainers helped him to develop a diet and treatment plan that enabled him to continue competing at the highest level. He won his fifth consecutive gold medal at the 2000 Olympic Games in Sydney, Australia.

Of his diabetes, he says: "At first I went into a denial phase—you do not want to accept that this thing is happening to you—and took as little insulin as possible. But after some months, I ended up taking as much as I could, always keeping in mind the maximum permitted dose. It isn't rocket science—frankly, it's pretty straightforward. Nevertheless, the level of ignorance is amazing. That's why I'm keen to promote greater testing and to tell people that coping with diabetes is as much about controlling your lifestyle as it is about health." (*Balance*, May/June 2001)

Redgrave tests his blood-glucose levels six or seven times a day with a small, handheld device that fits into his briefcase. Regular testing enables him to tailor his dose of insulin to the amount of glucose in his body and to the energy he requires. Needless to say, he needs a lot more energy when he is rowing than when he is watching TV.

Continuous activity

Since winning his gold medal, Redgrave has taken part in an almost continuous schedule of athletic, educational, and public events. He has played golf alongside Tiger Woods and attended a birthday party for boxing legend Muhammad Ali. But Redgrave has never been one to brag.

Redgrave believes that the best way to prove yourself is to show people your skills rather than talk about them.

"If you're the best in the world, that's good enough—it speaks for itself. So there's no reason to make more of it by mouthing off. The best way to prove your ability is by winning the race. Sport is very black and white in that way." (*Balance* magazine, May/June 2001)

Steve Redgrave (center) has won five Olympic gold medals despite his diabetes.

Emotional Distress

Diabetes does not cause depression. But living with any serious, long-term condition can be distressing, and diabetes is no exception. Everyone has ups and downs in the way they feel about their diabetes, and it is quite natural to feel fed up about it from time to time.

Anxiety and depression

At least one in five people become clinically depressed at some time in their lives, whether or not they have a serious condition. Many more experience periods of feeling miserable, which can have many different triggers, such as problems at home or at school, stress at work, or the breakup of a relationship.

Research has shown that anxiety and depression are more common in people with diabetes. This may be due partly to the changes in blood-glucose levels that they experience.

Family and relationship problems are normal, but having diabetes can add to a person's anxieties.

If they are depressed, people with diabetes may neglect their blood tests, injections, and diet. This can make their diabetes worse which, in turn, makes their depression worse.

Stigma

For people with diabetes, there are added factors that may make them anxious or depressed at times. They may be finding it hard to keep good control of their blood-glucose levels or they may be upset or embarrassed by having episodes of hypoglycemia. Despite the fact that diabetes is so common, some people still feel that there is a stigma attached to the condition. They feel that they are somehow labeled as different, abnormal, or unreliable.

Feelings of failure

If they are overweight, the need to diet and miss out on favorite foods may be depressing for people with diabetes. Having to increase the dose of drugs or add more treatments may also be depressing. It appears to indicate a worsening of the diabetes or a failure to control it effectively.

The appearance of complications of diabetes is another depressing milestone for some people. Many people develop eye, foot, or circulation problems even when they keep their glucose levels under reasonable control. This is distressing, too.

Depression is treatable. Talking about it with a doctor, counselor, or other therapist helps people come to terms with and develop strategies for coping with the problems that are triggering the depression. When talking on its own does not seem to be helping, a course of properly prescribed antidepressant drugs can be helpful.

"Every time I tested my blood sugar and wasn't able to achieve the results that I was wanting to achieve— even though I was doing everything I could—my self-esteem would be knocked down another step on that ladder."

(Nicole Johnson, Miss America 1999, *Health Talk*, Diabetes Education Network)

Pancreatic Transplants

A pancreatic transplant involves replacing some or all of a diabetic person's faulty islets of Langerhans cells with healthy ones that will produce insulin. Until recently the operation has not been as successful as other transplant surgeries such as kidney, heart, and liver transplants. But doctors have made important progress since the mid-1990s in transplanting islet cells from donated pancreases into people with severe type 1 diabetes.

The Edmonton Protocol

In 1995 researchers working in Edmonton, Canada, reported an important advance. They had extracted islet cells from donated pancreases from people who had died and injected them into the liver of people with serious type 1 diabetes. The technique—now called the Edmonton Protocol— is surprisingly simple and can be carried out under local anesthetic. Using a fine needle, the cells are injected into the main blood vessel of the liver. After the transplant, people are usually able to go home within 24 hours.

The Canadian team chose the liver rather than the pancreas for their islet transplants because the liver is better at repairing itself and building new blood vessels and support tissue. Once the islet cells have been injected, new blood vessels form around them inside the liver. This makes it easy for the insulin that they produce to get into the bloodstream.

Researchers all over the world are now experimenting with the new technique. The initial Canadian results were very promising, and patients experienced good glucose control after their operation. However, researchers need to check the long-term effects of surgery over several years before they can recommend it more widely.

Since the islet cells come from donated pancreases, the people receiving them need to take drugs to prevent them from rejecting the cells, which are different from their own. These antirejection drugs have side effects, so doctors use as low doses as possible.

Pig donors

A shortage of human donors has also led scientists to look elsewhere for islet cells. In the 1980s, Swedish doctors used pig islet cells to treat diabetes in human patients, with some success. Since then, researchers have been breeding pigs that have been genetically altered to make their cells more like those of humans. This makes their organs, including their pancreatic cells, more suitable for people. There is less risk of the cells being rejected and destroyed by the human immune system, which defends the body against infection.

Can Modern Science Cure Diabetes?

Diabetes is only likely to be cured if doctors can find a way to correct the underlying mechanisms that cause the condition. For people with type 1 diabetes, that would mean preventing their immune cells from attacking and destroying the islet cells in their pancreas that make insulin. Alternatively, some way to help them to produce the hormone would need to be found.

For people with type 2 diabetes, a cure would mean preventing their cells from becoming resistant to the effects of insulin. There needs to be a way to stop their islet cells from becoming exhausted by their body's increasing demands for the hormone.

Using genetic research

Finding and correcting the abnormal genes of people with both types of diabetes—so-called gene therapy—would be an attractive solution. However, gene therapy is proving difficult enough for conditions that have only one faulty gene, such as cystic fibrosis. Correcting the various abnormal genes linked to diabetes is currently beyond the abilities of today's scientists.

Instead, scientists hope they will gain greater understanding of how immune cells destroy islet cells in type 1 diabetes. Then they may find ways to suppress their destructive activity. Identifying diabetes genes would still be useful because it would help doctors to target their treatments to those who need them most. They could check newborn babies for faulty genes for type 1 diabetes and then give these children drugs to stop the destruction of their pancreatic cells.

Uncovering the genes that make people more likely to become obese—and to get type 2 diabetes—will help to target treatment for this condition as well. Researchers are trying to find the body's control switches that break down in type 2 diabetes and lead to gradual failure of islet cells. They also need to determine how environmental factors, such as diet, exercise, and obesity fit into the picture. Someday, doctors may be able to use drugs to reprogram the control switches so that people do not develop type 2 diabetes or can be treated as soon as they start to show symptoms.

Whose responsibility?

Doctors and scientists have made enormous progress in understanding diabetes. But, as the number of people around the world with diabetes moves steadily toward the 200-million mark, there is an urgent need for better treatments and for more widespread education about the dangers of becoming overweight and obese.

Many of those in developing countries hope for a more Western lifestyle, with fast foods, fast cars, and easy lifestyles. But they come at a high price to health. Experts predict that, over the next twenty years, the biggest increases in diabetes will come in the developing countries of Asia, Africa, and South America.

The cost of treatment

New treatments for the growing population with diabetes will be expensive. Already, millions of people in the poorer parts of the world cannot afford many important medicines, such as those needed to treat AIDS.

Genetic tests to identify people at high risk of diabetes will require expensive, high-tech equipment. The prices of new drugs to prevent islet cells from being destroyed in type 1 diabetes or becoming insulin resistant in type 2 diabetes will reflect the hundreds of millions of dollars spent on their research. Islet cell transplantation

Fast food restaurants are opening up in countries such as China.

will be available only to those who can afford the surgery and the drugs needed to prevent rejection of the precious new cells.

Prevention not cure

In the long term, preventing diabetes is the best option, especially for those living in poorer countries. If health workers can find those at high risk at an early stage—when their weight and blood-glucose levels are just starting to rise—they can help people to change their lifestyle so that they do not develop full-scale type 2 diabetes.

This type of screening and education program requires time and money from healthcare providers. Also, people at risk of diabetes need to decide to change their lifestyle. But if people do agree to take charge of their health, they may be able to avoid a lifetime of medical treatment. They can prevent serious eye, kidney, nerve, and heart diseases that could limit their everyday activities and shorten their lives.

"Governments can and must contribute to the battle . . . by encouraging and facilitating lifestyle changes, providing health education for all, and investing in primary prevention programs. There can be no doubt that now is the time to act."

(George Alberti, president of the International Diabetes Federation, 2002)

Information and Advice

There are many organizations that can offer advice and information about living with diabetes. Some can offer a counseling service to provide support for people with the condition. There are also diabetes organizations that work to find a cure for diabetes.

Contacts

American Diabetes Association
1701 North Beauregard Street
Alexandria, VA 22311
Phone: 1-800-DIABETES
Website: www.diabetes.org
The American Diabetes Association is a national organization that provides information and support to people with diabetes and their families, health professionals, and others who want to know more about the condition.

Juvenile Diabetes Research Foundation International
120 Wall Street
New York, NY 10005-4001
Phone: 800-533-2873
Website: www.jdf.org
The mission of the Juvenile Diabetes Research Foundation International (JDRF) is to find a cure for diabetes and its complications through the support of research. The JDRF is one of the leading funders and advocates of juvenile (type 1) diabetes research worldwide.

National Diabetes Information Clearinghouse
1 Information Way
Bethesda, MD 20892-3560
Phone: 800-860-8747
Website: www.diabetes.niddk.nih.gov
The National Diabetes Information Clearinghouse is an organization that serves as a diabetes information, educational, and referral resource for health professionals and the public.

Diabetes Action Research and Education Foundation
426 C Street, NE
Washington, DC 20002
Phone: 202-333-4520
Phone: 301-654-3327
Website: www.diabetesaction.org
The Diabetes Action Research and Education Foundation is an organization whose goal is to support and promote education and scientific research to enhance the quality of life for everyone affected by diabetes.

Websites

Children with Diabetes
www.childrenwithdiabetes.com
This website is geared toward promoting understanding of the care and treatment of diabetes, especially in children.

The Diabetes Monitor
www.diabetesmonitor.com
This website features an extensive collection of resources and links to other websites related to diabetes.

More Books to Read

American Diabetes Association, ed. *American Diabetes Association Complete Guide to Diabetes.* Alexandria, Va.: American Diabetes Association, 2002.

American Diabetes Association, ed. *Getting the Most Out of Diabetes Camp: A Guide for Parents and Kids.* Alexandria, Va.: American Diabetes Association, 2002.

Bryan, Jenny. *Living with Diabetes.* Chicago: Raintree, 1999.

Geil, Patricia Bazel, and Tami A. Ross. *Cooking Up Fun for Kids with Diabetes.* Lincolnwood, Ill.: McGraw-Hill/Contemporary, 2003.

Ginsburg, Art, and Nicole Johnson. *Mr. Food Every Day's a Holiday Diabetic Cookbook: More and Easy Recipes Everybody Will Love.* Alexandria, Va.: American Diabetes Association, 2002.

Olson, Michael. *How I Feel: A Book about Diabetes.* New York: Lantern Books, 2002.

Roemer, Jean Betschart. *Type 2 Diabetes in Teens: Secrets for Success.* Hoboken, N.J.: John Wiley & Sons, 2002.

Whelan, Jo. *Diabetes.* Chicago: Raintree, 2002.

Glossary

abdomen
lower part of the body extending from the chest to the pelvis that contains all the digestive organs, such as the stomach, intestines, liver, and pancreas

amputate
cut off a part of the body, such as a limb, in a surgical operation

anesthetic
substance that lessens or removes feelings and sensations, including touch and pain

anatomist
expert in the structure of the human body

bacteria
microbes that can cause infection

blood-glucose level
amount of glucose in the blood

blood vessel
small hollow tube, including arteries, veins, and capillaries, that carries blood around the body

carbohydrate
chemical compound that contains carbon, hydrogen, and oxygen. Carbohydrates are the main source of energy for animals.

cell
smallest unit of living things, including parts of the human body, such as the pancreas

depression
feelings of extreme sadness, hopelessness, and lack of energy

dialysis
technique to purify the blood for those whose kidneys do not work. Their blood is passed through a large machine that removes toxic substances

digestive enzyme
protein that the digestive system uses to break down food so that nutrients can be absorbed into the bloodstream

enzyme
substance that helps a biological change happen or happen more quickly, without being changed itself

epidemic
disease that affects a large number of people and spreads rapidly

ethnic group
group of people who share a common culture, tradition, and sometimes language

gene
part of chromosomes that carries instructions for how the body develops and carries out life processes

gene therapy
method of changing one or more genes in cells, usually as a treatment for a disease

genetic engineering
science of changing how a living thing develops by changing the information in its genes

gland
small part of the body that produces chemicals such as insulin

glucose
type of sugar widely used in animal cells to provide energy

hormone
substance produced in the body that influences how the cells and tissues function

hypoglycemia
abnormally low levels of glucose in the bloodstream

insulin
hormone that enables glucose to move from the bloodstream into cells

insulin resistance
condition in which cells no longer respond to insulin

islet of Langerhans
cell in the pancreas that produces insulin, which controls glucose levels in the body

kidney
organ in the abdomen that controls urine production and blood pressure

metformin
drug that is used in the treatment of type 2 diabetes

microbe
microscopic living thing. Microbes include harmful types of germs such as bacteria and viruses.

nerve
long, thin threadlike structure that carries messages between the brain and parts of the body. This allows the body to move and feel pain and other sensations.

obese
excessively overweight

pancreas
organ near the stomach that produces insulin and enzymes that help the body digest food

protein
large molecule made up of hundreds of thousands of amino acids linked in chains. It is needed for growth and to repair damaged parts of the body.

reservation
area of land in the United States that is kept separate for Native Americans to live on. Not all Native Americans live on a reservation.

screening
method of finding out whether a group of people have a disease or condition by asking them to go to a clinic for one or more tests

side effect
unwanted and sometimes harmful result of using a particular type of drug

sulfonylurea
drug that is used to treat type 2 diabetes by increasing insulin production by the pancreas

support tissue
tissue that surrounds nerves and protects them from damage

urine
fluid produced by the kidneys, which contains the body's waste products

Index